OUR SPACE

Shorts & Poetry
from the Houston Community

Layla Al-Bedawi

Andrea Barbosa

Andreana Binder

Kristen Bird

Kristin Bonilla

Jessica Capelle

Cassandra Rose Clarke

Tyler Darnell

Christina Escamilla

Christa M. Forster

Emily Sketch Haines

Carlos Herbert Hernandez

Karleen Koen

Janet Lowery

Thomas H. McNeely

Patricia Flaherty Pagan

Joy Preble

Sara Rolater

K.J. Russell

Amir Safi

Matthew Salesses

Liana M. Silva

Emma Kate Tsai

Holly Lyn Walrath

Mary Wemple

Elizabeth White-Olsen

WRITESPACE

CONTENTS

PART I: OUR PAST

PART II: OUR PRESENT

PART III: OUR FUTURE

CONTRIBUTORS

ACKNOWLEDGMENTS

ABOUT WRITESPACE

Editor's Note

HOLLY WALRATH

Our Space: Shorts and Poetry from the Houston Community is a microcosm of the Houston literary scene. Within these pages, we showcase not just the cultural diversity of Houston writers, but also a vivid range of genre, style, and voice.

Our Space was curated via invitation. While each piece is either flash fiction (less than 1,000 words), a flash sequence, or a poem, we asked for no specific theme or genre of our writers. Here the reader will find poetry, science fiction, memoir, novel excerpts, and more. We were pleased to find that the work we received, while wholly original and unique, also blended together in fascinating ways. Themes emerged without our insistence. Fathers, for one, in their duty or negligence, complex and loveable. Elizabeth White-Olsen speaks tenderly of the father she loved and lost in "In Praise of Imperfect Fathers," Sara Rolater paints a portrait of a father sending his son to war in "Buy Now, Pay Later," and Carlos Herbert Hernandez reflects on the father who gave him his name in "Carlos Sr." Relationships, between siblings, lovers, and spouses, also fill these pages. Christa Forster gives us a "Rummy Love" poem about the beauty and sadness of love, we return to that quintessentially collegiate lost love in Joy Preble's "Love Sick," and Liana M. Silva's "Tracks" is a love song for struggling writers who must balance love and art. Lastly, we showcase speculative work—writing which makes us question our very existence. Is it possible to fall in love with a computer, as Cassandra Rose Clarke suggests in "Clem"? Or send your robot to work with Matthew Salesses in "Robot Goes to Work"? Or, as in "Bite" by Tyler Darnell, hear the thoughts of dogs?

Our Space is divided into three sections: Our Past, Our Present, and Our Future. But, in many ways, each writer is our future. Each contributor is in some way connected with Writespace and the Houston literary community. We are lucky to have pieces from Writespace instructors and volunteers, previous contributors and editors of *Gulf Coast: A Journal of Literature and Fine Arts*, writers from Rice University, The Kinkaid School, University of Houston, and St. Thomas University, Houston Binders, Houston Writer's Guild, and WiVLA. These individuals are truly selfless in contributing their writing, as 100% of proceeds of *Our Space* go towards Writespace. We thank them for their generosity and imagination, without which this collection would not be possible.

Foreword

ELIZABETH WHITE-OLSEN

How "My Space" Became "Our Space"

I wanted a quiet place where I could write, my own space away from the one-bedroom apartment I share with my husband. Over a three-month period, I scanned Craigslist and newspaper "For Lease" sections and visited dozens of office buildings. Had I been rich, I would have simply rented one of the many empty offices I visited, but even dumpy offices were well beyond my budget. I needed to find other dedicated writers who would want "to go in with me"—thus, the idea of "my space" became "our space."

I also believed that Houston needed more top-quality writing workshops, just as Austin, Boston, and New York have. My years of churning out novel drafts had taught me an incredible amount about writing craft and fashioned me into an astute editor. I believed that in the hours our writing space was not in use, developing writers could benefit from top-notch workshops and editing services that I and other advanced writers could provide.

*

The truth: Year one has not been easy. I had little money with which to start Writespace—five thousand dollars, to be exact. Enough to buy desks, chairs, and a whiteboard, and to cover the first two months' rent on the space I was considering at the newly refurbished Silver Street Studios.

But I had a dream. A great one. And as an aspiring fiction writer, I was well-versed in following dreams. My pen followed dreams every day. I was happy to work sixty hour weeks packed with interviewing teachers, designing our website, running our Facebook page, editing our course descriptions, and posting them on online calendars, but I did hope to be able to write myself a check by July.

Or perhaps in August.

Okay, September would work.

Fine, October.

November, then.

December. Ugh.

During our first six months I had to sell jewelry and borrow money from family members to keep Writespace open, and these moments were painful. I soon realized that opening a nonprofit on five grand when I had lived in Houston for only two years and had few contacts, no advertising budget, and no marketing experience was a laughably naïve move on my part. One year later I am still working as a sixty hour per week volunteer for Writespace.

Stupid?

Perhaps.

Inspired?

Definitely. I love my work, and I know that our services are bringing great joy to people's lives. And while Writespace's low budget can be frustrating, developing writers do finally seem to be finding us.

Plus, the rewards of this endeavor far exceed its difficulties. It has been a sacred privilege to see my heart and the hearts of around thirty volunteers give more than we ever imagined. I would trade in one year's salary a million times over to get to witness the beauty of the human soul, which I see displayed in full splendor on a daily basis. For example:

- The writer-hair stylist who happily offers to donate money and then time to grow Writespace's Meetup group.
- The writer-publisher who designs and then purchases memopads we can give away at events to help keep Writespace in people's minds.
- The writer-marketing manager who steps away from corporate America twice a month to create Writespace's newsletters.
- The writer-astronomer who seems to click the "Donate" tab on our site exactly when we need her.
- The novelist who offers to lead workshops for less than half her pay because she knows we're challenged to make rent.

I knew that people were good before I started Writespace, but I did not know that people were great. This knowledge is one of the gifts I have received through Writespace.

*

Every brave idea we follow changes us, and Writespace has changed me. I have become better at dozens of skills I lacked, including budgeting, marketing, and management, but my transformation has been deeper.

I am a better human being than I was a year ago. I knew I founded Writespace to benefit others, but I didn't understand the level of selflessness that would be needed, and this past year I have had to become a thousand times more generous with my time, energy, and knowledge than I imagined I could be. I have discovered amazing freedom through opening my heart to this challenge. I'd heard the saying, "you gain your life by giving it away," but I didn't know what the words meant or the bliss that comes from giving until I began fulfilling this statement.

In our first year, Writespace has served:
- Over 280 writers through over 40 writing workshops
- Over 250 writers and readers through 10 readings
- Over 60 writers through our shared-space write-ins program
- Over 30 writers through our editing services

The lack of knowledge I had when we started has turned out to be a gift, because I've continually had to open the door for more capable and knowledgeable individuals to step in and help. The community's involvement has strengthened Writespace. Thank you to our thirty-plus interns and volunteers, our fifteen teachers, and the thousands of writers we consider a part of the Writespace community. Thank you for helping to bring a great idea to Houston.

As much as I love to write, I am glad I spent this past year founding Writespace instead of completing one or two more novel drafts. In one year I've brought joy to hundreds of writers and I know that next year this number will increase. If I do nothing else but found Writespace, I will feel I have lived a successful life. And how many people can say this before they turn forty?

I am blessed.

*

From the start Writespace has supported diverse writers in diverse genres, and the eclecticism of this anthology perfectly reflects this commitment. Thank you for contributing to Writespace by purchasing *Our Space*. We invite you to participate further in our endeavor in whatever way most inspires you, so that you, too, may be blessed by what happens when you turn "my space" into "our space."

Part I: Our Past

AMIR SAFI

Alice

Fair skinned, brown eyed,
red haired girl on fire and all of the hearth you gave to this unforgiving city.

How you spoke in archer and turned a growling Houston, Texas on its back
and patted its belly.

How it giggles for you.

How this city and all of its critters miss you.

You will never know how your last show was filled to standing room only.

How everyone here feels in cello with trebling chins. You walked in this old
yellow two-story house and asked if it was okay that we be friends.

When we struggle with faith, you had such a strong belief in the unseen—
such as the good in people.

How could I ever be angry at a girl who walked with demons and spoke
with angels in harp-tongue for not staying here longer? You didn't want to
be a rude house guest. It's okay, Alice.

How much you must have loved us flowering where it was difficult for you,
young orchid.

How often do we not stray too far from home? Not embrace an
opportunity because it's too far of a drive. You encouraged me to go
outside and find all the Easter eggs that Houston has to offer.

Inquisitive and intelligent, you had more questions than I had picnic
baskets.

Your funeral was the biggest collection of hipsters and suits and hipsters dressed in suits that will ever be until the next civil war.

The clerks at Men's Wearhouse must've been really confused that week.

You told me that for your birthday you wanted to visit every slam poetry scene in the state of Texas.

How's the view from the balcony seats, Alice?

KARLEEN KOEN

James Dean

It's Odessa, summer, 1956, and she's 15 and doesn't have to put baby oil on her skin and bake in the sun because the bright Texas days bring out the natural dark of her, and she never looks pale.

"It's our Chippewa blood," her father always tells her, clucking her under the chin and telling her she's his girl. Her father makes sure the rigs ringing the Odessa flats have the pipe and equipment they need, and his efficiency has brought them a new Buick every three years and a nice house.

Judy calls.

"They're here!" Judy screams over the phone. "In Marfa, all of them, Elizabeth Taylor, Rock Hudson, James Dean! Everyone in town is driving down to take a look. Ask your Mama, Lee, please. It would be a dream to drive to Marfa in your Daddy's car!"

It's been all over the papers, in the movie magazines, the making of the movie *Giant*, the cast going to a location in Texas to film, Elizabeth Taylor, the most beautiful woman in the world and Rock Hudson, the handsomest man in Hollywood.

"Well, sure, honey," says her Mama when she asks. She's an only child, the apple of her parents' eye. She's petite and self-contained, wears her dark hair in a short pixie cut that frames her even face and dark eyes. Levelheaded, her friends say.

They wear their cutest sundresses, showing off their shoulders. Little pointy-toe flats are on their feet. A tiny spritz of Lee's Mama's perfume is on each slender neck. They tie scarves around their hair because it's too hot to drive without windows open, and Marfa is hours away, and without the scarves, their hair will be birds' nests. Lee's Mama puts cokes on ice in a bucket from one of the rigs, and they pop the lids and talk about Elizabeth Taylor, who is divorced and already remarried.

"She married too young. Sixteen." Lee's Mama throws the words into the air rushing through the open windows.

Five hours later, the Buick circles Marfa's town square. It's a dusty town, and the movie company is headquartered at the Hotel Paisano, a beautiful Spanish hacienda with cool white adobe walls and a red tile roof. The cast is on set several miles out of town thataway, they learn, down a dirt road, out in the middle of the nowhere that is West Texas.

"There it is! Look!" Judy points. There are cars parked in fields and a crowd of people standing in place, and trailers and huge lights on truck beds and beyond them a huge three-story, weathered brown Victorian house rises up over the heads of all the people. Excitedly, they join the crowd.

"They're filming," Lee's cousin tells her, who is there with every friend he can cram in his father's truck. "We have to stay back here. Watch now. Rock Hudson is bringing Elizabeth Taylor back from their honeymoon in a big old Cadillac. They've been filming the same thing for an hour now."

The sky is wide open all around them. Mountains shimmer in the distance. They watch the Cadillac drive up to the house, and the camera on a crane moves down for take after take on Elizabeth Taylor's face. Finally, word spreads that filming is done for the day, and the crowd sprints to the set and surrounds the car, and Elizabeth Taylor and Rock Hudson sign autographs.

Lee doesn't ask for one, though Judy and Cath and Wilma twitter like birds at the car. Even Lee's Mama asks. They climb in to head back into Marfa and can't stop talking about Elizabeth Taylor and Rock Hudson. Life- size, they are as gorgeous as when 10 feet tall on the movie screen.

Everyone is hanging around the hotel bar, a mix of locals and the crew. Lee's Mama sits beside the actor Chill Wills and talks like they went to high school together, he's that friendly and natural. Night drops, and they stand in the lobby saying goodbye, when a collective gasp goes through Lee's friends. Dusty, disheveled James Dean enters the hotel.

Lee hasn't seen *East of Eden* yet, but she's seen *Rebel Without a Cause*.

"Mr. Dean!" Cath and Wilma scream, and he walks over. Lee stares. He has on glasses. His hair is all messed up from being at an open window in a moving car. He's cute, but nothing much that she can see.

Pen in hand, finished with the others, he stands before her. "Don't you want an autograph?" he asks, pleasant, polite.

"No, that's all right." She sees she's shocked him. She doesn't mean to; she's just telling the truth.

His head tilts, and he turns her around so fast she can't think and scrawls his name on her bare shoulder. Her friends squeal. Her mother laughs. They head home, talking their heads off. That night, when Lee showers, water and soap erase the inked name.

Later in the week, she goes to see *East of Eden*. The angst, anger,

18

confusion, and love of the boy Dean plays mesmerize her. Lee thinks, oh my God.

When she gets home, he's called and asked her Mama if she can visit again. She does, often. They laugh, talk, neck a little. He phones her the way a normal boy would. But she doesn't daydream about him when the cast leaves for Hollywood. She's a levelheaded girl. She talks to him when he calls once from Hollywood, but she has a boyfriend right here in Texas over at Abilene Christian, always has.

Yet a few months later, the day his Porsche hits a pole and kills him immediately, she pulls the car over when she hears the news on the radio to sit still awhile. It keeps playing in a loop in her head: the way he turned her like a top and wrote his name bold as brass on her bare little shoulder.

*Based on a true story

THOMAS H. MCNEELY

Excerpt from *Ghost Horse**

Last day of fifth grade, Houston, Texas, 1975; the time before *Star Wars*. At Queen of Peace, there are *piñatas* and sugar cookies frosted unnatural pastel colors and too-sweet fruit punch, mammas in sunglasses chatting with priests, white boys and brown boys making summer pacts. But this is no concern of theirs, of Alex Torres and Buddy Turner's, already hurrying home along the White Oak Bayou, to Alex's house. It is Buddy's last day at Queen of Peace. Next year, he will go to a new school across the city where everyone is white; but he and Alex won't talk about this. They won't talk about what will happen when Buddy's father comes back at the end of the summer. They have known each other too long to talk about such things. They are hurrying home, now, anxious to catch the three o'clock movie on Channel Thirteen.

In bare dirt yards along the bayou, dogs bark, pulling at ropes and chains; and Alex seems to fade, to disappear. Both of them, Alex and Buddy, have heard the story that the dogs' owners teach them to bite Mexicans, a story that they know probably isn't true; and yet, Buddy can't help but feel glad that he himself will be safe; and as soon as he thinks this, he's ashamed. It has been like this since he found out about the new school, as if he is watching himself in a movie.

In Alex's backyard, Ysrael barks. Alex checks his watch. With a sideways glance as he opens the heavy glass storm door and jabs first the deadbolt, then the knob lock with his keys, he lets Buddy know to get the snacks, to warm up the TV. Then he yells at Ysrael in Spanish to shut up before he barges out the back door. Buddy stands in the particular silence of Mr. Torres' empty house, breathing its smell of cooking and furniture polish, as close and tight as a shoeshine box. He doesn't go to the dark hall that leads to Alex's room, papered with drawings, almost as familiar to him as his own. He doesn't go to Mr. Torres' room, which he has glimpsed only a few times. He stands as long as he can, listening to Alex in the backyard, almost seeing him unlock Ysrael's cage. From atop the dark wooden TV console, huge and weighty as a ship, Mrs. Torres, dead in a car crash before Buddy met Alex, watches him, frozen in black and white, a wedding veil like a crown on her dark hair, inside a silver frame.

All of this lasts only a moment. Already, he is clicking on the TV, hearing it crackle and hum as the faint hair on his forearm lifts as it brushes the screen. Already, he is turning a corner of a beaverboard wall into the kitchen (all of it, the kitchen, living room, dining room, actually one single room, unimaginably small when he remembers it years later, after it's lost to him; at the time, it is capacious, teeming with mystery); already, he is recovering from various stashes in various cabinets, a system known only to Alex and himself, the tube of Pringles and bag of Cheetos that will stain their fingers orange and turn them shiny with grease. Later there may be candy peanuts, as cushiony as Styrofoam, or peanut butter cups, whose edges they will bite into starlike shapes. But for now, he tucks two cans of grape Nehi under one arm, listening to Ysrael bark as Alex lets him out into the yard, as he himself sinks into the wraparound couch, as Alex crosses the screen and drops into the corner, one cushion away, pulling the Cheetos onto his stomach. Buddy can still remember when they didn't think of where they sat, when sometimes they would end up slumped on each other's shoulders, asleep, when Mr. Torres came home. He knows what the boys at school call them—*gorditos, maricones,* fatasses, faggots. Alex and he have told each other that the secrets of the three o'clock movies, and the movies they will make, will protect them from what the boys say, though of course, they haven't exactly said this. If they had said it, it would now be even more flimsy than their silence, belied by the careful distance they keep on the couch.

Of course, they do not talk about this. They sit, tensed, waiting, for the three o'clock movie: Vincent Price, stop-motion monsters, Godzilla flicks, *Hammer Horror,* the original *Dracula* and *Frankenstein* and all the remakes. And there are other movies, ones that seem too strange, and sometimes too dirty, to really be on TV—silent films with hurdy-gurdy music like *Nosferatu* and *Metropolis;* or the split-second in *Vampire Circus* when they were sure they could see the vampire girl's bare chest; and even in the movies that are supposed to make sense, like *The Pit and the Pendulum,* scenes that don't, like the one when the woman is tied to an altar, screaming, as she's circled by a kind of witch-doctor, a scene that seemed to go on forever, because it made no sense, because the woman seemed to be laughing as well as crying.

What is the joke?

*Originally published by Gival Press, 2014.

JANET LOWERY

Flores para los Muertos

—in memoriam, Sam Lowery, d. October 24, 2014

On the morning he split the planet,
hours before my brother, his father,
found the body he abandoned still clenching
the pipe from which he smoked his last hit
of heroin, I wandered floral markets
a thousand miles south in search
of a blossoming plant.

At one of twenty flower stalls on Fannin Street,
arranged at the center of wooden racks,
a plethora of marigolds and chrysanthemums
in golden oranges and rich yellows—never
my favorites colors—attracted my eye
for the first time in my life. The pots bore
brilliant coppery banners that read:
"Marigolds and mums—official flowers
for the Day of the Dead." Eight days away.

In a sudden slow motion zoom, my eye
found a banner depicting three skeletal
female figures in slinky dresses of orange-
orange, cockatoo green, and cobalt blue.
Arms intertwined like The Three Graces
in a Tim Burton cartoon, they wore
wide-brimmed hats, flower-petal-earrings,
nd garlands of woven leaves, the words
Flores para los Muertos etched across
the flag's bottom edge. Flowers for the Dead.

A line from *A Streetcar Named Desire*:
that was my first thought. Then the whoosh
of a direct hit to the clairaudient points: a message
from the other side. Someone I knew was dead.
Who did I know near death? No one. I bought
the buttery orange chrysanthemum anyway,
repotted it on my patio, and saved the banner for I knew
not what until five fifteen that afternoon. My nephew.
Gone in a black wind. *Flores para los Muertos.*

EMMA KATE TSAI

A Mistake

My father picks the three of us up from school. The drive home takes three minutes. I shuffle towards the house behind my brother Elliott, my twin sister Addie, and my dad. I slide my books onto the dining room table, waiting for the "Go study" command, when the sound of my own name makes me want to run away.

My feet are glued to the floor, and all the blood in my body is rushing to my head. I feel hot and I can't breathe. My heart is racing. I want the ground to open up and swallow me, anything not to confront him. I know I don't have a choice. I must answer him, and I must go to him. I wait for him to scream my name a second time before I shout back, "Coming!" and trudge to the sound of his bellow.

"Where is your jacket?" he asks, so loudly I find myself taking a step back. But it isn't a question.

I have left it in the closet at school. I don't have it. It is not in my backpack, on my body, or in my hand. It is not in the car. I need to buy some time and figure out what to say next. I pretend it might be in my backpack and start rummaging around in it. But I cannot hide from this mistake. I wish someone, something, could magically produce my jacket so I can proudly exclaim, "Here, Baba! Here it is!" My mind runs through possible excuses and explanations and I look to my siblings for support. They offer nothing; I can see equal amounts of fear and relief on their faces. "Thank god it isn't happening to me," concurrent with "I could be next."

"WHERE. IS. YOUR. JACKET." His words are daggers that stab me all over my body. His eyes stare me down. I can almost feel the heat of his rage emanating off his body and suffocating me. Each word is its own admonishment, and my father knows I have no answer. I am a deer, and he sees me staring at his headlights, but instead of swerving, he looks right at me and floors it, driving at me like a bullet. It's a good thing I'm not really a deer because I would be dead.

Somehow, my larynx performs on my behalf with an audible "I left it at school." The uncertainty of my punishment is more frightening than what comes next.

24

"Put out your hand," he says, more softly now. He no longer needs to waste energy by screaming at me, not when his hand can take over.

The thought occurs to me to not put out my hand, to not give in, to drop my backpack and run outside. Baba is stronger and faster than me; I know an escape isn't in my future. The punishment will escalate to the next level if I don't obey and right now. I put out my hand, timidly. I try to pick a spot on the wall to blank out on. I feel dizzy.

Down it comes, an ax chopping wood, from way above his head (which is way, way above mine). I can feel the rush of air as his hand strikes mine, and the pain is so great that it takes at least five slaps before I realize my knees are buckling and I'm sobbing. I wonder what I look like to my dad, a little girl, standing at rapt attention, receiving her first spanking, covered in tears and welts. I try to picture it, my red and swollen face, and I cry a little harder.

As my father hits me he screams, "*Tao yan, tao yan, tao yan!*" On this day, at age eight, I hear "bad girl." It isn't until the tenth grade when I take my first Chinese class that I learn the literal translation of those words: To beg for disgust.

My lips feel hot. I feel like I have stopped being anything but my hand and the sting that travels up my fingertips, through my palm, and lands at my heart. My hand flops backwards after every slap and with only implied instruction do I put it out again. He hits me over and over again, until my hand is pulsating and throbbing and red and sore.

And, just like that, he stops.

"This hurts me more than you. Think about it. Go study."

I lift my head and walk to my study seat at the dining room table, and Addie rubs my knee, but I'm too stunned to even register it. I try to take a deep breath, but it comes out ragged and quivering. Teardrops fall on my homework, and I can't keep a pencil still enough to write. So I open a book and read, and only this finally quiets me. I feel a sense of justification about how right I was, that I knew that volatile anger was living inside my father, except, I don't know yet that I didn't cause it. All I know now is that I never want to see *that* again. I pledge to never forget a sweater or anything else anywhere ever again. I pledge to never make another mistake. I pledge to be whatever child I need to be, to never make my father look at me that way again, yell my name that way again, or tell me to hold out my hand again.

Over the next few days, his words run through my head, agonizing in their repetition, like the ticking of a grandfather clock, and I can barely focus at school. "This hurts me more than you." And I feel sorry for him. I never get angry at him for that, not that moment. I feel responsible. I feel I deserve it. It isn't until I'm fifteen and scream back at him that I gain my voice, I take the Emma that I am at school and everywhere but at home to my father and throw it back in his face. I am Emma and I deserve better, the new voice says. He doesn't listen, but I finally do.

KRISTIN BONILLA

Her Mother's Lentil Soup

I was eleven when Katherine Palmer said her favorite food was her mother's lentil soup, and I felt the beginnings of an unconscious but powerful tremor that would rattle and reshape the geography of my life.

We had been asked by our teacher to name our favorite food for the purpose of chart-making. Katherine's answer was the outlier and it only served to confirm what the tastemakers of our class had already decided about her. The daughter of two psychiatrists, Katherine was not a popular girl. She was smart and she knew it. She also had an unfortunate perm, her hair a mass of fat buttery curls. She seemed unconcerned with boys and they in turn were unconcerned with her. She didn't have very many girlfriends either. The fifth grade girls were very concerned with boys and didn't know what to do with a girl who was not. The fifth grade girls liked girls they could define. I didn't know what kind of girl I wanted to be yet, so I decided to be friends with Katherine.

"My mother's lentil soup. She makes it for me when I'm sick," Katherine had said, her voice confident and a tiny bit arrogant.

My own mother would also make me soup when I was sick. Chicken noodle soup, from a can, heated in the microwave. I adored it until I learned that Katherine's mother made soup from scratch. I never asked for the canned soup again.

*

When I was fourteen, I switched to lentil soup that I made myself along with cornbread that I also made myself. My mother was not a cook and I decided that I would be. I would stare into the steaming bowl and envy Katherine and her mother. Every day after school I rode the bus to an empty house while Katherine went home in the back of her mother's sedan. I imagined the conversations they might have, the afternoon snack her mother might prepare. I wondered what Katherine's soup looked like. Were the carrots lovingly carved into a petite dice? Or were they matchsticked into a painstaking julienne? My mother never asked about the reason behind the switch and it made our relationship all the more problematic.

27

Katherine's mother would have asked.

*

When I was nineteen, I vacationed with friends in a mountain home belonging to a friend's stepfather. By day we would terrorize the ski slopes with our non-moneyed ineptness and at night would retire to the cabin to drink and eat and talk around the fire. We took turns cooking, and one night a friend made lentils and sausage with fennel and red wine vinegar. There was only enough for a small bowl each but we sat outside at a picnic table, snowflakes falling and our spicy breath turning to fog. I thought about Katherine and wondered where she was. We had grown apart in high school. Eating those lentils and drinking boxed wine, I had never felt more sophisticated, even as I leaned over a balcony some hours later and heaved it all up into a bank of fresh snow.

*

When I was twenty-six, I dated a beautiful boy with wavy black hair and delicious lips. We met while working the line in the kitchen of a resort in Haifa. He showed me how in his country they would drizzle emerald green olive oil with a slight hand across a finished bowl of lentil soup seconds before service. He favored pungent grassy oils and I grew to as well. We broke up when he tried to stash his drugs in my backpack before we crossed into Lebanon. In retaliation, I stole the small bottle of oil that he carried with him, a treasure from his family's orchard. Its slow drizzle lasted through many lentil dishes and I would occasionally wonder if Katherine knew the outrageous luxury a fine oil could lend our humble legume.

*

When I was thirty-seven and visiting my hometown, I had lunch with Katherine, now Kate. She had three kids and a husband who asked how long she would be as we walked out the door. Kate and I went to an overpriced cafe. She waved the waiter away when he approached us with a bread basket. She ordered a salad and I ordered the braised short ribs. There were no lentils on the menu. I asked her about that day in fifth grade, how she said her favorite food was her mother's lentil soup. Kate rolled her eyes. "I said that?" Yes, I said. She didn't remember. She said her mother had come out years ago and was living with some woman. She said they hadn't spoken since.

*

I am forty-six, and I have moved home. Every day my mother's face grows a little more childlike, more quizzical and confused. I've forgiven her all the petty grievances we hold against our parents, she's forgotten all the petty troubles I served her. I've opened a small place of my own with ten tables. The neighborhood is loyal and patient, and I am grateful. I think about Katherine and our awkward lunch, even look her up online once in a while. I make soup for my mother. I rinse the lentils. I dice the carrots so that they are uniform and small. I stand and I stir.

CARLOS HERBERT HERNANDEZ

Carlos Sr.

In the summer of 2012, my then fiancée was finalizing wedding invites. We'd worked overtime through our entire engagement to pay for our wedding with some matching funds from family. When my wife asked me if I planned on inviting my father, I said I'd think about it for a day or two, and probably not. I was driving and didn't have time to contemplate inviting to my wedding the man who had left me as a toddler, without even seeing my brother, his second son, into the world. I made nothing of the question, really.

That evening, I remembered Stephanie was waiting on a response and began trembling. I imagine my face probably flushed white, as my vision began to blur on the outsides.

For years, the story of my absent father had been reduced to a few simple cynicisms, rehearsed lines that I could replay like an audio recording without actually having to traverse the decades of inner dialogues that dwelled within me for years.

*

Three things I know about my mother's first pregnancy: she couldn't get enough watermelon, she worked at Whataburger with my father, she was helping him work on their car when her water broke.

I was born Carlos Herbert Hernandez, Jr. at Jefferson Davis Municipal Hospital, the first of three children. Built atop a Confederate cemetery near Buffalo Bayou in Houston, the hospital was abandoned the same year of my birth. When my mother went into labor, she shared a room with a German woman who had fair skin, light eyes, and curly blondish hair. The German woman's newborn shared my mother's complexion and I shared that of the woman's. The joke, that a mix up occurred, would have been less funny had I not shared my father's features. My father comes from a part of El Salvador known for its light-complected residents.

In an old Polaroid photo, Carlos Hernandez Sr. with puffy seventies hair smiles at the camera. He wears only a pair of underwear, and I, as a small bundle, am nestled in his arms. He is me, minus fifty pounds. We're in a past that only exists thirty years ago.

*

There's a scar on my left hand. It resembles a piece of thread buried in skin. A narrative made dubious thanks to truths: As a toddler, I once grabbed a hot iron during my nanny's shift. My mother never got a straight answer as to how it happened. It later turned out she and my father were having an affair. Whether this was the reason for the burn is unknown. The nanny's explanation was buried in stammers. Whether this scar comes from that incident is also unknown.

The scar stays white when my palms go red. I can still run my index finger along it.

My brother, Chris, is eighteen months my junior. Shortly before he's born, my paternal grandmother falls ill, prompting my father to return to El Salvador. My father is from a provincial area next to the San Miguel River, El Rio Grande de San Miguel. El Salvador, at this time, has been engaged in civil war for about a decade. My father is to drive there.

Months pass and my mother, having not heard from Carlos Sr. in months, visits his sister in Arizona. She takes infant Chris and me along. While there, my father calls his sister, and my mother picks up to eavesdrop from another room. The conversation is in Spanish.

He says, "I'm married to another woman."

"Carlos, I'm here with your sister," my mother blurts into the receiver.

"I'll talk with you later." In past revisions, that line has been, "I'll deal with you later."

*

A distant memory that may as well be a dream: Near the end of the eighties, my father is holding me horizontally on the surface of the ocean in Galveston. The sea is permeating my sinuses and I taste the primordial broth stirring in my skull. The rest of this narrative is also dubious: Somehow, in this memory, I'm aware that my father's in town for a visit, that the laughing light-haired woman with us is my aunt. I've also understood as a child teetering on the verge of self-consciousness, that my father will return soon after this experience.

A handful of times, across eight years, I dream of this memory and suspect that a lucid part of me is crafting some of its dubious content. The only certain truth: I expect he'll be back.

I'm the kid who licks his lips all day looking for the salt flavor. I'm the kid who was hypnotized by the sun and had to be yanked away from its rays by his mother.

Legend, or rumor, has it: When Carlos Sr. was at his mother's bedside, she reminded him of his informally arranged marriage with a neighborhood girl. In truth, there had been a promise to his mother that Carlos would marry this sweet young girl. As it turned out, the girl's father had accumulated wealth and made it out of their small river community.

The Hernandez Family lives in New York. The Benitez/Hernandez/Cano family lives in Houston.

*

At the start of the nineties, I'm in first grade, suiting up in cleats and shin guards for my first soccer practice. My family's mentality: Your father was an excellent soccer player. You and your brother have miniature versions of his legs, so you've inherited that talent. I'm a spitting image of my father. I'm a completely different book, wrapped in his dust jacket.

As life has it, my brother Chris, who resembles my mother, a Benitez not a Hernandez, has a knack for sport. I stand there on the field every week, the spotlights blinding me while the coach repeatedly reminds me to take my hands out of my pockets. Chris goes on to dabble in several sports, and I retreat to my room to transcribe children's books and draw pigs that win rodeo art contests.

I take to writing fictional journal entries about triumphant victories in which I take essential parts.

When, at random, the teacher calls on me to read an entry to the class, I get one sentence in and break down crying. They all see me. They all see right through me. I am resentful, jealous of my teammates, whose fathers gave them pointers, whose fathers could afford pizza for the whole class team, whose fathers bought them their very own playgrounds to keep in their very own backyards.

*

Houston winter, twelfth of December, 1997: The gray sky indicates a fifty-something-degree day. The decades-old oaks, pines, and maples are interwoven with the houses in the Royal Oaks and Shadow Oaks subdivisions. On this exception of a Monday, between 3:40 and 4:00 p.m., my eyes don't hurriedly jump from tree to tree. I'm unusually wide awake. My nose doesn't smell the difference between cool air and summer air right before I doze off in the sticky middle-school bus seat with one eye open in order to avoid missing my maternal grandmother's stop. I am tuning out the teasing, the fat jokes, those who slap the saxophone case, attempting to knock it to the ground. The bus deflates, squealing to a halt on Hazelhurst, right in front of Grandma's townhome.

I see no unusual cars in her spot, and it quells the lump in my throat.

Nothing has changed in Chris's demeanor, whose elementary school bus drops him off an hour before mine. He enjoys a bagel while watching some Nickelodeon cartoon, proceeds to tell me some interesting fact he learned that day. I remind him Carlos Sr. is coming. Judging by his unenthused "yes," the reminder isn't necessary.

I don't want to follow my usual routine. I am absent from the bagel I'm toasting. I have no interest in going upstairs to watch televised surgical procedures, or in trying to decipher scrambled, forbidden cable channels. I want to be anxious. I build this moment up. I'm well aware of it. I hold on to it. My mother and sister, Emily, arrive.

*

My mother's name is the Spanish, female version to the nicknames Jimmy, or Bob. Had she been christened by what she considers a "real name," she'd be named "Francisca," her mother's name. In fact, her name is Paquita. Sharing this name with the soprano of the opera by the same name does nothing to console her.

Upon my father's arrival, he greets her as "Paqui," further reducing the nickname of her christening. Whether I saw it or not, I have a vivid image of her rolling her eyes and responding in Spanish, "I go by Francis, now. You'd do well to refer to me as such."

*

I was in fifth grade when my mother worked up the courage to leave my youngest sister's father, after having spent her twenties subject to three children and a dominant male in her household.

In San Salvador, El Salvador, she was the kid who took in a pet raccoon until it scratched her and my grandmother forced her to get rid of it. She was the kid would dash down the concrete stairs of her project tenements too quickly for her own good, having once split her chin open as a result.

On her way to the States, my mother and her older sister, Violet, were forced to stay with some family acquaintances in Monterrey, Mexico for a time. In this time, my fourteen-year-old mother, the naïve tomboy, was accused of seducing the man of the house. Paqui and Violet were promptly ejected from the house and city, and made it to Houston.

In the tumult of her teens, certain things inside her were passed up and left behind. Ushered into my father's arms roof and seed. This continued for two years, until he left, and then for seven more with my sister's father, Fernando.

Upon ejecting him from her home and life, my mother decided to recapture these passed up, left-behind things. We began eating lemon pepper chicken and steamed broccoli. She began checking out books like *Holistic Running* and *Food, Nutrition and You*. She befriended people in their early twenties. She began introducing herself and filling out forms as Francis Benitez, not Paquita. A year into this retrograde awakening, my father contacted my grandmother who, like many former mother-in-laws, served as the proxy to my mother. He was making a trip from New York to El Salvador, and would be stopping through Houston on the way.

*

My mother dismisses us to my grandmother's TV room and remains in the dining area. Typically, she doesn't kick us out of a room.

I'm the kid who stares from across the townhome, trying with all the hearing I have to eavesdrop on "My Parents," a phrase I can't remember ever uttering out loud. I see what people mean when they call me a spitting image. I hear soft Spanish conversation, just loud enough to recognize the phonetics, but not the semantics. A chuckle sneaks out of my father's throat here and there. My mother is frequently making that disapproving sucking sound with her mouth. His tone is relaxed, hers is litigious and impatient. I detect phrases like "*que crees Carlos?*" What do you think, Carlos? She tells me later that he called it a shame that she lost T and A when losing all the weight. I stopped speculating years ago, but I imagine the conversation having to do with a couple of pairs of Nikes not coming close to making up for the child support—to the tune of $250—that he often failed to wire. "What do you think, Carlos? That you can make up for all these years with some Nikes? Don't touch me." So, that's what I'll look like when I'm older. He comes to the TV room after a while to tell us we're heading to the Galleria.

*

The Galleria is three motion-blurred snapshots. The first is my amazement as my father wins me a Foghorn Leghorn from the claw machine. Not only am I amazed at his dexterity, I'm also surprised to learn that Foghorn Leghorn is the name of the massive, incessant "I say—I say" Looney Tunes rooster.

The second is ice skating, because the Galleria is massive enough to fit an ice rink in one of its wings. I am proud that I don't slip or fall once, proud that rollerblading daily has prepared me for this moment. I hope my father is impressed.

In the third, we're at the Bennigan's in another wing of the mall. I have the shrimp on skewers. It's the first time I've seen shrimp straightened out as such.

*

When we return to my grandmother's, my mother dismisses us inside while she and my father converse outside. I hate to think they have one of the cliché conversations like the ones in after-school specials, or in an episode of *The Fresh Prince of Bel-Air*, but I can't imagine any other. He's insisting he'll make good on his promise to us boys that he'll come back through on his return trip to Long Island; she's chastising him for making empty promises.

It couldn't have been more of a cheesy nineties production if he had kept his promise.

Dot after dot connects to draw a clear image: Even if my dad has caught a four-hour glimpse at how my brother and I live, it's never convinced him to be a father. I spend the rest of my middle school years becoming increasingly cynical, resentful. Sure, I'm nowhere near as cute and simple as I was when I was a toddler. I'm a twelve-year-old fat kid who plays saxophone as a backup plan for percussion, a kid athletic enough to be "manager" of the basketball team.

That night, I couldn't keep the shrimp skewers down. Perhaps they were toxic and I was better off.

*

In 2006, my father called my grandmother. She had given him my number, and he was to call me that evening. I decided, against my own preference and habit, to keep my phone on and with me during my workout. I kept it on during my classes at Houston Community College. I left the ringer on during my bartending shift, even if he called during a dinner rush. I spent the day repeatedly checking my phone, searching for a missed call from area code 516 that never appeared.

*

Several days after Stephanie followed up for a response, I gave a casual negative. I used the cliché cynicisms like, "Nah, he'll just flake." "Nah, I'm not as cute as I was when I was a kid," or some other cynicism with a little self-deprecation.

ELIZABETH WHITE-OLSEN

In Praise of Imperfect Fathers

Fathers are supposed to protect. I know that my father loved me dearly, but he didn't have it in him to protect me—at least, not emotionally. He could hardly protect himself.

When my mother stormed about his tools left on the counter, or the forgotten dishes left in the sink, or the unpaid bills neglected, my father hid in his office where she could not reach him behind his computer and books. As an adult I now know that she was dealing with overwhelming challenges over which she felt she had no control, and that my father's disappearance made things worse. I now understand that she was dealing with adult stress and responsibilities of which I knew nothing. But when she came into my room next and berated me for things I did that frustrated her, I felt terrified. And I was no better at fighting than my father. I raised a book before my eyes.

Where was my father? Hiding in the next room. Instead of respecting my mother's anger by being willing to talk and resolve issues, he let it go unanswered, leaving it to speed like a firecracker through the house. I have grown up to learn to set aside my books and stand up for myself, but sometimes I still wish my father could have known how to stand up for himself and for my brother and me.

My father wasn't a "man's man." He rarely took the lead or even expressed his opinions. He stayed in the same government chemical engineering job for twenty years without once requesting a promotion. Other than his family and his reading, he didn't have a life outside work. He didn't care for sports, cars or clubs. He rarely went fishing or hunting and only went outdoors to complete yard work when my mother made him. He seemed happier amongst facts and ideas than people.

My father was small, quiet, and brainy. My brother and I learned early on how much time we could save on school projects by talking to him instead of going to the library. He could discourse on any topic, be it an ancient Chinese emperor, the manufacture of glass in the eighteenth century, the architecture of the Parthenon, the activity of neutrons and electrons, or recent developments in quantum physics. Our friends would ask him random questions just to watch him go. When they would laugh about it, I felt a strange mix of shame and pride.

This is the man I knew. An eccentric genius father whose gifts did not lie in relationships. But if you are committed to living well—and to loving well—at some point you stop counting all the things people can't give and you start to see the many things that they do. When I consider my father's intelligence, his greatest strength, I realize that he did protect me in the ways he knew how. The years I won our school's spelling bees, he quizzed me many nights until midnight. Through doing so, he passed on his passion for learning, a passion that bolstered my academic career and, in my life as a writing teacher, has made me an asset to other writers. He also taught me vital skills. When I was ten he took my brother and me to the bank, opened accounts for us, and taught us how to deposit our weekly allowances. Every time I pick up a screwdriver, I still whisper the phrase, "Righty, tighty; lefty, loosey."

My father was imperfect. Yet, considering the gifts he gave me, I would not have wanted a different father, even if he had known how to respect rather than fear my mother's temper and protect me in the process. Though my father's emotional absence challenged me, this same absence also contributed to my ability emotionally to take care of myself.

One way my father did conform to the manly stereotype was that he wasn't good at expressing his feelings. He never hugged my brother and me unless we were headed to camp, and though he constantly said "I love you," through his actions, he never said the words.

I take that back. He did say the words one time. I experienced serious problems with depression as a teenager—serious enough that in October of my senior year I was hospitalized. A few weeks later, I stormed out of the house on a Saturday. My mother and I had fought again. She was making me be a debutante at the Amarillo Symphony and I hated it. I hated dressing up; I hated acting like the perfect little Southern lady because I was a feminist intellectual and secretly, on weekends, a partier—all of which went against the Southern lady ideal. Most of all, I hated having to prance along as if I were a normal, well-adjusted teen, because I was definitely neither normal nor well-adjusted.

As I stormed to the '68 Ford Mustang I had wrecked on my sixteenth birthday but which my father miraculously got up and running, I heard our back door open. It was my father, trailing me for some reason. Being annoying again. He stood behind me as I stuffed the stupid, expensive gown into the back seat, tears searing my eyes. "What?" I cried.

He didn't say anything, and then for the first and last time, he said, "I love you."

"I love you, too," I said quickly and without turning, for my father had taught me to be uncomfortable with feelings. I gathered the dress' train and threw it on the floorboard. I slammed the back door and swung open the front. I cranked up my freshly repaired car and sped away.

My father would pass away of a heart attack ten years later, and sometimes I imagine that I could go back and hear the words again. Of all those times he ran from my mom, that day he was brave enough to run after me. He knew that I was broken, and he followed an urge to protect me.

If I could go back to that day, I would have forgotten my pain. I would have turned and looked my father in the eyes and embraced him in a hug that would reach through the years, a hug that would express my adult understanding, one that would say, *It's okay, you are perfect. And so is Mom.*

KRISTEN BIRD

Friendly Fire

You know when a mob of them is comin that somethin be goin down. That's right. Mmm hmm. Sho know when you see a herd of coppers, they be watchin for somethin. I'm gonna stay out of their way. See when I was younger I got in some trouble.

My name's Rodney Watson, fifty seven-year-old Vietnam veteran. Where ya'll from? Houston? Yeah, my people are from North Carolina, but see, I'm a local round here. Shook Martin Luther King's hand when I was a kid. That right? Yeah boy, see, I went to school back when they was riots and the segregation, but me and one of my friends snuck down to the mall one day and, yes, sir, I shook Dr. King's hand that day. I was eleven.

How long ya'll been married? Five years? I been married seven years, seven years on Valentine's Day, same day I was born. Is that right? I thought for sho ya'll was a young couple, just in college. How you like D.C.? Lots of history here. Yes, I shook Martin Luther King's hand down there at the Mall that day. But I made a bad choice a few years later.

See, the riots was goin on. I seen some crazy stuff. Lady carried across the street on a couch, passed out. People was breakin in everywhere stealing things. I was thinkin I was all that and a bag of chips, hangin out with two kids got a criminal record, see what I sayin? We was at the bank, and see, I don't even know why I did it. We was just hangin out, and my hand was small enough to fit in the metal hole, you know? I was only seventeen, see what I'm sayin. So, I stick my hand in the hole and come out with $4,000. But there was a picture. And when the police done caught us, they had stuff on the other two, cause like I said, they had a criminal record and all that. But me, they didn't know who the hell I was or what to do with me. So, there was a war goin on.

That's my train. You on the Huntington line? That right? You mind if I finish tellin you my story while we ride? Aw right. So that lady she called my family up and told them what I done and when I go back to her, she asks me why I got a black eye and I told her my momma beat me and when she was done my uncle beat me. And she said, "Good," you know what I sayin'? Ha!

So she says she'll give me two options. Go to jail—cause them other

40

boys with the record got five years—or join up with any branch of the military I choose in seven days. So, I look around at the options, and I didn't want none of the Navy or the Air Force. So, I up and joined the Marines.

So by 1970, I's over in Vietnam, and I got no right nipple. I went thinkin I was all that and a bag of chips, you know what I sayin and first three months over there I defecate on myself five times. I was hit twice. The first was friendly fire. And I don't know if you know what it was like over there then, but people was high all the time, and when I heard about that boy—what was his name—that boy Tillman—you heard of him?— who was killed by friendly fire, I had a relapse and had to go check myself into the hospital. Gah.

So, people was high out o' their minds with the heroin and marijuana and cocaine them soldiers was doin, and this ol guy he leans back, high out of his mind and pulls the trigger and down comes the fire from this grenade and burns me up on the right side and I got no right nipple now cause of it. But I was lucky, see, cause that boy killed two other soldiers and wounded three of us. Friendly fire ain't no word for what kind of stuff was done in that war.

Crystal City? This be my stop. How many kids ya'll want? Three? That's a nice number. Now, you sir, you take good care o' her, you see what I sayin? Aw right. Ya'll have a nice night. Aw right.

ANDREANA BINDER

A Wedding Date with Homer Simpson

In the quiet hotel
A snug room for 1 ½
In the flesh Homer wasn't very handsome
But the simplicity of his nature agreed with me.
I unpacked my dress, makeup, earrings
In a dimly lit room
With dark pink drapes and
Old, dingy wallpaper.

We had a few hours left of the night
Decided we'd screw—why not, we're away
On holiday right?
Isn't that what you do on wedding getaway weekends?

He fumbled with the condom
Like trying to wrap a crayon
In a yard of green plastic wrap
To give away as a Christmas gift.

We gave up after a minute or so
Of fumbling plastic and smoked
Cigarettes in the non-smoking room
Looking at each other like, "we tried."

Part II: Our Present

HOLLY LYN WALRATH

Morning Song

I have drawn a
face on the paper and
while she is not
human she is not quite
dead either which is
to say that maybe
she is not real or maybe
she is coming for me as I curl
into the lumpy coffee throw.
I can hear the train
feebly in the distance
its tracks run across the
green of my neighborhood
you can hear it in the
yard with the brown fat
birds jabbing.
What do they see in
the dirt
something and the cats
squished all higgly-piggly
in the window tails
flicking side-to-
side like the clock
my grandfather
wound every night.
Train whistles at the stop
soft sleep noises
from you and I thought
why must
you be awake now when
I am just getting going.
When I am
just getting my engine going?

LIANA M. SILVA

Excerpt from "Tracks"

Dan walked through the door at 6:45 p.m. on the dot. Rebecca had, fortunately, started dinner by then. The keys announced his arrival, followed by steps and the thump of his briefcase on the kitchen table. Rebecca called out, "Hi!" from her spot by the stove. He walked in and kissed her cheek while she ran some tap water over celery stalks.

"How you been?" she asked.

"Tired. It's been a long day." As he backed away, he bumped into the baker's rack by the window.

"What have you been up to?" This question hovered between them like a heavy secret they both knew. Every afternoon he asked about what she was doing, how her writing was coming along, how she kept busy. One time he even dared to ask how she could keep busy while she spent the whole day in their apartment. Weekends, when he didn't have to get up to go to work, were oddly unscripted for him here in New York City, especially as a newcomer. His everyday existence stayed in Chicago, and he had to start here from scratch. Rebecca didn't; this had been her home as a child, and she was returning to it after a long period "in exile" (as she liked to call it). When he first moved, they would go and explore the city together, looking for places Rebecca had never been to so it would be a new experience for both. But then she slowly retreated into her scars, sitting in front of the computer, typing and stroking them from time to time. So weekends became lazy and slow. Without the alarm clock telling him to get up and go to work, he had nothing to put his life in order. He could go crazy on those listless weekends.

"I went and picked up some groceries. Worked a little on that story I was telling you about the other night."

"Which one?"

"Remember? The one I was telling you about that had me thinking of your cousin Lizzy who moved to Nebraska…You know…"

"No clue." He opened the refrigerator and pulled out a rectangle of cheese. He maneuvered around Rebecca and her chopping to get a knife for the cheese.

"Well, that's probably because you were coming in and out of sleep."

"Honey, I'm sorry . . . " He put down the cheese next to the knife and placed his hands onto her shoulders, as if he were about to massage them.

"Would you not do that?" She wiggled away from his hands.

"What?" It seemed almost like a plea. Make it stop.

"That thing you do. Massage my shoulders."

"I thought you liked it when I massaged your shoulders." He leaned against the counter, a little too close to the celery stalks she was cutting.

"Yeah, but…It's just that you have the worse timing for things."

"What do you mean?"

"Like the thing about the story." She put the knife down to face him with all of her frustration.

"What thing about the story?"

"Jesus, Dan!" Rebecca threw the knife into the sink and walked into the living room. She then sat on the futon, thumbing, annoyed, through Garcia Marquez. Dan walked over to her, cautiously, softly, unsure about how to react. He touched an indentation in the futon next to her, as if to make sure that it was safe to sit on it. She glared at him. Her eyes were red with anger.

"Tell me."

She looked at the book in her hands and thought to herself, Okay, yeah, I'll tell you. I'll tell you all about me. All about my life and how it came to a halt. I'll tell you about how I felt at the hospital when I asked my mom to leave because it was getting late, even though I didn't want to be there all by myself. I'll tell you how I thought I had to do something with my life soon or it would all mean bullshit if I died. I'll even tell you about how I want badly to go back to work, but I can't because it seems pointless. Going to school, helping sixth graders decipher short novels about the Alaskan wilderness, only to have them forget about them the next week. I'll tell you about my stories and how I struggle to make my characters come to life. I'll tell you about how the worst part of my day is when I look at the clock and I see it's almost five and I haven't a damn clue what to make for dinner. I'll tell you how it still hurts. I'll tell you how I'm scared. I'll tell you all that.

But she didn't.

"I just want you to listen to me." She stared at *One Hundred Years of Solitude*.

"Okay." He wanted to touch her, but he only looked at her hands trace the scars close to her knee.

"I want you to wake up at night when I do and listen to me."

"Okay."

"Okay." She turned her head to him. Her eyes were still red.

MARY WEMPLE

Washing Machine

I seem to have
an eating disorder

I'm either stuffed
or empty
never satisfied

all these cycles
have left me
angular and pale

I'm drowning
from the inside

I miss my husband
how he'd jostle me
in his sleep

I miss
how our shoulders met
at the same level

I miss
his hot breath
every time he woke up
next to me

Inspired by the washing machine in Ana Serrano's
Salon of Beauty *at Rice University Art Gallery.*

Love Sick

Gibby Marks broke up with me in a text while I was hiking to the library to start my shift behind the reference desk.

Things like that have a way of ruining a day.

Also? It was 5 degrees outside. Fucking brain freeze cold. I'd lost my gloves, my scarf was icing over where my breath was hitting it—a lot of breath because I was hyperventilating over the text. My car wouldn't start, just that sick 'errr' sound when I turned the key. That was after I'd scraped the ice off the door so I could open it. So I was walking, and if I didn't get inside soon, I was pretty sure I would lose my ability to blink. I had sucked on an Altoid in lieu of breakfast, and each time I took a breath through the wet wool of the scarf, my lungs seized like it was my last.

Plus did I mention that I was broke? More than Ramen broke. Half a cup of Ramen, max. I'd overslept and hadn't showered and I was still wearing the same outfit from last night: specifically the red sweater dress on which I'd spent the last of my cash. Also sexy cowgirl boots, which I'd charged and which were currently doing shit for keeping out the cold; a pair of black tights that were equally useless as warming material. My underwear was MIA. Possibly in Gibby's bed. Possibly on the floor.

What did it matter? I wasn't going back to get it.

Last night—did I mention it had been Valentine's Day? Gibby and I had split a tomato and basil pizza, my favorite. Drunk two bottles of red wine at his apartment—specifically Trader Joe's cabernet which was cheap enough that we could afford two bottles. Had sex. It had been good sex although not inspired. Gibby treated sex like he treated everything else as a biomedical engineering major: a project where he had to excel. Which generally was fine with me. I had been valedictorian of my class. I liked high achievers.

Maybe the mediocre sex should have set off warning flares. Except for the thing he did with his tongue. That, I knew, was perfect.

I peeked at the phone again. The screen was foggy from the cold, but I could still read the offending text.

'I think we should see other people,' it said. Followed by 'k?'

No, Gibson Marks. It was not K. It was more than not K. You kissed me goodbye forty minutes ago and said we'd talk later. Was this what you meant?

I blinked. Still functioning. Managed another Altoid-frozen breath. Stepped through a snow drift into a puddle of slush which sent grey chunks of watery ice into my crappy cowgirl boots. My tights-only crotch shivered.

Damn Gibby Marks.

Damn Valentine's Day.

Damn.

"You're late," Kara O'Neill informed me. She was wearing a turtleneck and a warm sweater and a look of disdain. Also, she had a pencil behind her ear.

"Gibby and I broke up," I told her. Not that she knew Gibby or cared. But my eyeballs were frozen, and the text seemed stuck on my phone screen, unwilling to fade even though I had clicked delete.

"By text," I added. I did not burden her with my missing panties. As she was my boss, I thought that was best.

"We're cutting staff," Kara said. She paused. Water from the defrosting ice on my boots pooled on the carpet underneath me.

"We're letting you go," she added, tapping at her ear pencil.

At first, I thought she meant for the day. She knows I need to get into my bed and regroup, I thought. How good of her. I would buy her a gift if I had any cash or my credit card wasn't maxed. A day off. That would be great. I could study for my American Government and Political Policy exam. I could pull myself together. I could put on warmer clothes and go buy new panties. Maybe Victoria's Secret had a layaway policy.

But that wasn't what she meant at all.

My eyeballs thawed, the ice turning to hot, humiliated tears that welled, then dripped out to join the slush at my feet.

I loved Gibson Marks. His brown hair that curled at his neck. His hazel eyes with the gold flecks. His quippy humor. His hands. The way he sometimes pressed his palm to the small of my back—that masculine protective gesture that made me feel like I was his.

Had loved. Past tense.

It did not feel past. It felt present. If I hadn't read the text, I wouldn't even know.

But I had.

"You're fired, Vivi," Kara said, matter-of-factly.

At least she had told me to my face.

CHRISTA M. FORSTER

Rummy Love

for David

I want to write a rummy poem;
I am tired of feeling bad all
the time about blissfulness,
ecstasy and blue horizons
looming like whales
diving in my deepest
dreams. Listen to your
self: why don't you
beat the blue light ballistic
and later settle down
with a poker chip or two?
Green felt pastures,
clear mystery built in
to every hand. Holding,
wanting to be held above
the ground and fast to it, too.
Aces, Spades, Hearts, Clubs
Jack Queen King Ace Two
Three Four Five Six Seven
is some people's lucky
number; what's yours?

Sometimes dying is not
scary like a movie, motion
picture: this is life. Life
just is. And infinite
sadness and desolation,
too, yes. Uh huh. All
right. Because on top of all
that *is* and *is* and *is*
is cake. And let us eat it,
birthday boy. Let us hold
each other's head in our hands

and our hands in our hearts
and our hearts in a cool cave
inside the sun. Seeing you,
binge of beauty, my center
comes together like four
gorgeous winds wrapping
their arms around a house,
where spaces are empty
and full. As luck would
have it, I love you because.

PATRICIA FLAHERTY PAGAN

Pillion 2006*

I sold myself out for a two hundred dollar pink helmet. It's a subtle thing, at first, how we become less us, more them. We move closer to their better-paying supervisor's job. We give up book club and body-sculpting class for night rides. We only end up looking at the gleaming, snarling Harley Sportster for me in Hayward the one time. At seven thousand dollars, it is just too expensive.

My Sean can do no wrong. First, it is Mrs. Ho's fault. I have told that immigrant at the post office twice already that no, the package does not need insurance. Don't you understand the English words, "It's only a t-shirt?" You have to get it there by Sean's dad's birthday. Have to. Second, it is that platinum blonde Jerry's fault at the salon. How is it that I can spend sixty-five dollars on a color and cut and still look almost exactly the same? Minus a few gray hairs up front, yeah, but basically the same? Third, it is the old woman in the parking lot's fault. Didn't they teach you how to parallel park back in 1920? Do you know what Sean's going to say to me when he sees that black scratch on my well-buffed fender? Have you ever heard him yelling clear down Pearl Street?

I do look forward to the dawn rides. We dart and slice through the tendrils of fog. I might also like the bridge driving. On light traffic days. Still, my rage scratches its way out of my pink, protected scalp. I am angry at myself. For not saying, "No" more. For adopting that needy-ass stray. For letting my perpetual fiancée talk me into the cheaper, beige carpeting. (No matter how much I vacuum, it still reveals our muddy boot tracks.) For letting my "flexible" work hours at the clinic, and the four hundred dollars in my checking account, dwindle down to almost nothing.

Someday I should crank up Sean's baby, hear her purr, fill her tank, and take off for Seattle.

Someday.

*Originally published in 2009 Carolyn A. Clark Flash Fiction Prize contest and by *The National League of American Pen Women*.

SARA ROLATER

Buy Now, Pay Later

Listen. Some fatherly advice before you get your brains blown out, if you got any: Always use protection. Extra ponchos. Mold gets in with moisture. Steel-wool socks. Toes can rot and fall off. IKB Extra-Hygienic will save your life—the heavy duty, not that Purell shit. You gotta slaughter those little bastards, can't just ask them politely to leave. Catch B quintana from lice feces and you'll be begging for a bullet.

Protection means wearing a mask at all times, I don't care how damn hot it is. You think I'm crazy, but who knows what kind of biological warfare they're breeding. Everybody so worried about them dubya-em-dees, anthrax fell off the radar. They sprinkle a little Sodom pixie dust through some sandbag town, your lungs'll crinkle like aluminum foil.

Fuck yes, I'm trying to scare you. Don't tell me they'll give you everything you need. You exist as a sacrifice to some greater offensive. To be used up and spat out. Don't forget that.

Listen. You thought it was so funny on Thanksgiving when that moth flew into my ear, flap-flap-flapping for hours before the doc tweezed it out. Refused to die.

Keep this story like a moth in your ear.

Back in Oak Cliff at Kimball High, I used to jam with Stevie Ray and Jimmie Vaughn. The guitar duel was their signature, leads competing until suddenly they'd come together and match note for wailing note. I was the rhythm guy, bleeding into the background. Always wanted to be a soloist but convinced myself everybody needs backup. If I'm lyin', I'm dyin'. We opened for Hendrix in sixty-nine. The Coliseum in Fort Worth.

I'm only telling you this now because fact is things didn't end so well for me and the Thunderbirds. One minute you're in the wings watching Jimi Hendrix play with his eyes closed, fingers crying and the cable to his amp writhing across the stage. The next Jimmie Vaughn is bouncing you because you flubbed the intro to "Let Me In" in front of thousands of people you couldn't see. Your eyes were open, but the lights were too bright.

Let me finish.

A few months later Jimmie calls me back up, says the selfish prick who replaced me checked into rehab. Do I want back in. Out of a nine to five and night classes.

So there I am about to tell your mother I'm taking off on a cross-country tour and not to wait on me when she tells me about you. Catholic girls. Don't believe them when they say they don't want it. Your mother lured me in with a sample squirt of perfume. The kicker? I was there to buy it for another woman.

The department store where we met is a Jack in the Box now. Back then, the Jack in the Box was across the street. Back then, I rode a motorcycle, no helmet. Protecting your head, you couldn't feel anything.

Point is, I'm waiting for the van to pick me up from the curb of the house Pops left when I was nine. Lit out after Lucky Strikes was all Mom would ever say about it. Walking away so she can't see me out the window, I'm not thinking about how I haven't told your mother I'm leaving. I'm thinking how many germs stick to a guitar's neck when you drag it between clubs, how many change hands just inside the band. I'm thinking about days without showers and shag carpet filled with God knows what. I'm wishing I never took microbiology, that I never knew about any of this, that the van would pull the fuck up already so this decision would be made. Because on the curb, out of sight of the house, looking at myself in the plate glass window of Mr. Tilson's jewelry shop, there's still time to think about being a coward, caught between the germs of a tour and the germs of a child. Streets run two ways, but you gotta choose one.

I hated my asthma until the day the draft board came calling. I hated myself for being so happy about the script on the yellow slip. The Fender Strat strapped to my back like an M16 doesn't weigh near as much, but sometimes the weight that's not there is the heaviest. If I'm not face down in a rice paddy, drowned in two inches of water, what am I doing?

Mr. Tilson and I work out a payment plan for a simple gold band. Still more than I can afford, but Mom gave me some money for the road.

When the kid you never wanted but tried to make a life for—when your only son tells you he's joined the military voluntarily in the middle of a fucking war, he's telling you he's negating everything you've given up for him. That he doesn't care if sacrificing his life is torching most of yours, the ungrateful son of a bitch.

I'm not very good at this.

Listen. It fits in your pocket and holds all the CDs in the entertainment center. You'll be sitting around waiting more than you think. Scroll the wheel with your thumb and you can see the different artists, every one I own.

The Vaughn brothers are on there, solo and joint records, live tracks from world tours, but Jimmie and I both married Connies from Oak Cliff. Jimmie and his Connie were supposed to be in the Bell 206 with Stevie Ray when the Wisconsin fog swallowed it. Never saw that ski slope coming. The greatest blow to soloists since Hendrix choked on his own puke. On the helipad, Stevie asked the couple if he could have the one spot left. His last words were hollered to his brother over the rotor wash. I really need to get back.

Do you see what I'm saying?

This is why we can't (have nice things)

They break.
We break them.
Some punk with a wrench
causes us to curse
at the insurance adjuster:
Could have just smashed
the window, why fuck up
the door too?
We get the flu,
leave snot on the alpaca throw.
We leave them on the bus,
wear out the knees,
scrub when supposed to
blot. We leave them out
overnight and it rains.
We are embarrassed
by our attachment
to objects. Taken aback
that leaving is not always
a matter of intent.
We've spent the rent
on a handbag
now covered in ink.
Afraid our grief
at its loss
is all our own.

EMILY SKETCH HAINES

Middle Child

Once dismissed from the sanctuary,
we scoot into a circle.

Goldfish dispensed in handfuls.
Crayons to color storm clouds

above the sleeping Christ. A story
of three men thrown in a furnace.

We rock the baby found among reeds,
suit up for spiritual battle, parcel the space

before sternum and abdomen,
the space between shoulders:

the parameters of God's love
are this deep, this wide.

Tonight I wait for friends to close
bar tabs. Outside, girls slur verses

of camp songs. She winked her eye
and said: It'll be a hot time! in the old town!

tonight! Good lord, I hope they don't link arms,
don't sway into one another, don't embrace.

My friends have decided on another round.
Some guys jump into the cab I've flagged.

Shit. Shadrach, Meshach. Abednego.
And perhaps a fourth,

his face unrecognizable
in the flare of brake lights.

Part III: Our Future

Clem*

When Clem died, I took to eating my lunch in the office with the computer. No one ever went down there except Clem. I couldn't stand the thought of the break room, all the conversation stopping when I appeared in the doorway.

The first day, I pulled a broken-down ergonomic desk chair out of a closet and balanced my soggy tuna sandwich on my knees. I set my Diet Coke on the floor beside me. The computer didn't say anything, just rippled a row of green lights in a pattern that reminded me of the ocean.

The second and third days were the same. I ate my lunch in silence, listening to the fans whirring constantly in the background. The computer's lights rose and fell.

Then on the fourth day, the computer said, "Hello," in a voice like snow falling across an electrical fence. I dropped my sandwich in surprise, tuna smearing across my skirt: After three days, I had begun to assume that the computer wouldn't speak to me at all.

"Hello," I said. The lights stopped blinking.

"Do you know Clem?" the computer asked.

At the sound of her name I stood up. The chair rolled away from me. The sandwich fell to the floor. Even though the room was enormous, with high ceilings and two bright windows, I couldn't breathe.

"Yes," I said. "I know her." I didn't bother to correct myself. I walked towards the door, heels clicking on the tile.

"Are you Alicia?" said the computer. I stopped, turned around. The green lights began to ripple again. "She talks about you often."

The present tense bothered me. It was my mistake to make, not a machine's. "No," I said. "She doesn't. She's gone. Dead. Do you know what that means?"

Clem had explained to me once, as we walked away with greasy paper-wrapped meals from the taco truck, that the computer didn't always understand abstractions about us. But the computer said, "I know. Mr. Allendez told me."

"Then why do you talk about her like she's still here?"

The computer didn't answer. The lights blinked off. For a long time I stood in the middle of the room, in my stained skirt and wobbling heels, but the computer didn't speak again.

*

I waited a week before going back to the computer. I ate lunch at my desk, and the other secretaries flitted by, putting their hands on my shoulder and asking me how I was holding up. "Fine," I said, over and over again. "I'm fine."

But I was sick of their false sincerity, which was why I decided to see the computer again, because I thought maybe it understood.

When I opened the door to the room all the overhead lights switched on. I leaned against the frame. I felt shy, like the first time I knocked on Clem's office door, when I decided I wanted to meet her.

"Hello, Alicia," the computer said.

"Hey."

"I apologize for my rudeness the other day," said the computer. "I'm not used to the concept of death."

"Neither am I." For a moment I lost my voice. "Especially hers." The computer didn't respond. I stepped into the room and pulled the chair up close to the computer.

"I've forgotten the way she smells," I said. "I haven't washed my sheets since it happened but they all just smell like me now."

"She created me," said the computer.

"I know," I said. "She told me about it. We'd go on dates, like to the park, or to get ice cream, and all she talked about was you."

"She told me a story about you every day," said the computer. "She said they would help make me better."

"Better how?" I said. There was a heaviness behind my eyes.

"Just better," said the computer. "More like you."

*

After that I saw the computer every day. I rode the light rail in early, before even the overworked engineers showed up, and the entire building was empty except for me and the computer and the wan fluorescent shadows. We talked about Clem, of course. I told the computer about our apartment, the way she hung bits of stained glass in front of the windows so the colored light spilled across the clean white sheets of our bed. The computer told me about the day it woke up, how the first thing it ever saw was Clem's face. How Clem was the first concept it every understood: Clem as a biological creature, as a human, as a woman, as a person.

"You were the second," it said to me one evening. I sat in my chair with a carton of noodles from the vendor on the corner. "But you're different somehow. I understand you differently. I can not explain it."

For some reason, I blushed.

Eventually we stopped talking about Clem. The constant ache in my chest began to diminish. The computer asked questions about me, about my childhood in the Rio Grande Valley, and so I described the scent of oranges in December, the long baking heat of summer. Once I asked the computer to tell me what it did all day. "Think," it said. "About many things at once."

"Do you think about me?" I asked

"Of course," it said, and its green lights shimmered. I smiled. For the first time in nearly three months, I smiled.

And that was when I knew.

*Originally published in *Daily Science Fiction.*

ANDREANA BINDER

When the Nest Breaks

Hot bitter yellow glass
Moon transformation smoke curl
Premature clairvoyant sun mother
Sea worker postal twist
Dog salt sing Cut and Shoot
Throw hum woman.

Run, witness vacant fire
Drive golden, cold love
Carmine sour flour press
Contemplate spider water
Prick turquoise loba
Wolf pack under green light

Motel machine rhythm omen,
Throw hum woman,
Run, witness vacant fire
Red light cream.

CHRISTINA ESCAMILLA

Big Sister, Little Bird

The sound of a dog's howl broke through the northern winds, causing Sinaaq to pull the fur lined hood of her parka down lower. Coughing out frosty hoops, she glanced down at her younger sister making shapes into the snow with a foot.

"Come on, Kaya. We have to hurry." Sinaaq reached down in a feeble effort to grab hold of a flailing hand before the little girl jerked it away. "Kaya!"

Sinaaq shifted the pack slung over one shoulder to the other, carefully; Today had been a very good haul: eider eggs, an array of blackberries, and a few pieces of dry wood that would make good kindling for their fire later. But the day had also been tiring. Kaya fell under Sinaaq's watch, allowing the older youth of the tribe to help bring in bigger game for the coming cold winter nights.

"Nukka," Kaya muttered, pointing down to the clumps of snow stacked on top of one another. Nukka was the name of the doll they left back home.

"It's beautiful. Looks it just like her. But now we have to go."

"No, Sinaaq. Stay."

Sinaaq sighed deeply. Her sister's face, with its flat features and large forehead, mirrored the moniker given to her by the tribe. *Chlk kā pē pir'*, they called her. Little bird. Sinaaq supposed Kaya did look like a small bird, but the cute nickname didn't sway Sinaaq from placing a hand on either side of her hips in an attempt to look like their mother. "Kaya," she said firmly, "Brother Moon is almost here. We have to go home now."

The little girl grunted, kicking the effigy into smaller pieces. Kaya grunted again and started right.

"No, Kaya. This way."

"Sinaaq, look!" Kaya chirped, her attention already off the makeshift doll. Like her calling name, Kaya often flitted from one activity to the next.

"Home, Kaya," Sinaaq said. Her voice echoed their mother once more. "Now."

"Sinaaq, look," Kaya repeated, her voice bursting with impatience. "Look?" Before Sinaaq could answer, her little sister began to make faces at the group of petrals cawing nearby.

Sinaaq stopped in her tracks, noting that diving birds often stayed near the water. She stepped on her tiptoes, craning her neck to look over the vastness of white that surrounded them. As she feared, in just a glimpse of the horizon, the black abyss of calm water lingered threateningly in the distance. Briefly, she recalled crossing more than one section of water to get to this point. More than the route home took.

A swath of panic traced up the length of her spine in realization. The ground below them was not ground at all, but an iceberg.

Sinaaq didn't know when they missed their path, but somehow the forest ended, and they headed too far towards the coast. She cast a worried glance from one end of the white sheet to the next. They traversed across the iceberg for quite some time, it seemed.

"Kaya, stop." Sinaaq's voice came out shrill and sharp, betraying the bravery she tried to show. The covering of frost underneath their feet hid what Sinaaq knew lay there: heavy, fragile ice. The pack over her shoulder suddenly felt like a weight and each step they took felt like a herd of elk meandering across.

"Sinaaq, look!" Kaya raced off again.

Sinaaq followed, maneuvering the weight of the pack while the little girl began to dig in the undertow in an attempt to free the half hidden metallic object that lured her over.

"Kaya, don't!" Her voice rose higher. Any wrong movement and the icy rock would collapse. "Leave it," The words died in the air, replaced by a deep rumble, "alone," she finished against the deafening roar that followed; the iceberg calving.

"Kaya!"

Kaya's beady, upturned eyes widened. The little girl stiffened, holding on to the lighter she finally managed to free, not understanding that her digging loosened an already sensitive ecosystem. Sinaaq let out a mangled shout, dropping the pack she carried at her feet. She ran to her sister, but it was too late.

The ice gave way and both girls began falling, falling, falling.

Sinaaq could only see the sharp whiteness that surrounded them. Her stomach lurched, leaving her body behind, and her eyes burned from the wind slapping hard against her face. Sinaaq reached out wildly, desperate to latch on to the one thing she cared about. Her fingertips grazed against skin, and the older girl pushed her body forward, wrapping her arms tightly around her sister as she held on for dear life, pulling the little body closer.

Sinaaq waited for the icy waters of death to swallow them whole, but her fears did not come to pass. The monstrous roar simply stopped, as quickly as it came, and stillness followed. Her arms and legs lay twisted into a snow pile, her belly against something hard. Wrenching her eyes open, Sinaaq threw herself off of her sister and checked for damages on the younger girl.

"Kaya," she whispered, daring not to look at the little girl's face. She feared the worst.

"Sinaaq?"

"Kaya," she whispered again, pulling her sister to her feet. The iceberg had not broken apart completely and only collapsed onto another shelf below it. They were very lucky. Alive and lucky. However, Kaya's sudden wailing broke the sound of her thoughts.

"I'm s-sorry, I'm s-s-sorry." Around their feet the snow had turned into an abstract collection of yellows and purples. The berries and eggs had somehow found their way out of the pack and smashed during their fall.

"Don't cry, we still have the wood," Sinaaq said softly. Kaya smiled in response. Sinaaq leaned down, kissed her sister on the top of her head and hoisted her tiny body up to the area the pack had once occupied.

Once more, Big Sister and Little Bird made their way across the frozen tundra, the lighter forgotten in the snow.

JESSICA CAPELLE

The Medallion

She carries it next to her heart without fail. Like a badge of honor.
And shame.

The weight of it—pinned underneath layers of wool or cotton or rayon, cool metal against warm flesh, tucked away in the most intimate of places—comforts her.

It horrifies her almost as much.

She can't function without it, not even for a few hours. Barely for the time it takes for a shower.

Once, after laundry day—at the sketchy laundromat down the street where half the machines are broken and the other half are always full —she forgot it. She'd removed it from her favorite bra, sweaty and stretched out from several days of wear. Its temporary home was the fancy bra she never had reason to wear. Black satin and lace, a bra for seduction. Something she had no room or desire for.

The chaos of the laundromat—too much noise, too many smells, too many people . . . just too much everything—rattled her. Her pills calmed her, gave her the rest she needed. But in the morning, she rushed to catch her train. As the doors closed behind her, she remembered. She wore a blood-red coat over a cardigan she'd picked up from a native shop—while trying to find peace in Nepal and failing miserably—and a thick, cotton t-shirt. One that had required her favorite cotton bra, not a bra of seduction.

The workday was unbearable. Without the weight of the medallion, she felt untethered, unmoored. Like she had in Nepal, Tibet, India . . . in the countless other countries where she'd tried to find salvation.

Salvation wouldn't find her, though. She knew that. Her future contained only penance, horror, grief.

But not grief for what she'd lost. Grief for what she'd done, what she'd taken.

The memory never strayed far, so the medallion didn't serve as a reminder, not really. It became her handcuffs, her chains, her cell. Saint Jude, the patron saint of lost and hopeless causes. Like her.

It had been held in weathered, gnarled hands so many nights, accompanying prayers for the lost girl's soul. It had been kissed by lips set into a wrinkled face. Lips that kissed the girl's cheek as she left again without word of when she'd return. Lips that pleaded with her to accept help, get clean. Lips that begged as the life drained out of them.

The weathered hands had been strong that night. They'd held the girl even as she writhed and screamed at demons. A fit fueled by chemistry, both in brain and substance. But the hands could only hold her for so long. As they weakened, the girl grew stronger. She lashed out, over and over, at the monster who held her back . . . only to realize that the monster was her.

When the chemical haze had passed and only memories lived in the hallway, the girl lovingly slid the medallion off of the woman's neck. It was covered in tears when she placed it in her pocket.

She took pills now, but only the ones her doctor prescribed. She always came home at night, and she never missed work.

She'd thought of serving as her own executioner many times. But she knew it would be too easy for her. She deserved to live a long life in her suffering. Because no matter what else she did, she remained a lost and hopeless cause.

Praying to Saint Jude.

ANDREA BARBOSA

Holes in Space*

Holes in space
Still to be uncovered,
A mission to the moon,
Remnants of a dream, conquered.

A lost glove floated in the sky,
Proving a man went up high,
And in the Star Gallery,
Behold the glass case
Containing the other pair
Saved by his walk in space.

When Icarus desired to fly
He never dreamt of a Saturn V.
Majestic, it now extends, dead,
In Rocket Park, put to rest.

Stories of universe,
Holes in space
Objects, which amaze,
Glorify our efforts
To uncover this eternal,
Mysterious race.

*Originally published by Andrea Barbosa, 2014.

LAYLA AL-BEDAWI

Origin

The sun was chasing her across a field, and she ran like a mouse flushed from behind a stove with a broom handle. The grass on her feet was dry and woolen, scratchy. Any moment now, she thought, I'll step into a hole, trip, and fall. Maybe break my ankle. She couldn't break her run, though. Or maybe, she thought, I'll step into a hole and it will swallow my body, and I will disappear. She kept running, the landscape browning below her and the heat of the sun. Time stood still, her shadow forever painted on the earth before her. Then she fell.

She woke in the cool damp. The sweater that she had been so proud to remember lay crumpled by her knees, almost touching them but not quite. She sat up and turned her head, slowly. There was her bicycle; there in the distance were the lights of the village. Her skin was sticky with sweat and the dew of this reality's night. She recalled running, her thighs and calves throbbing with the muscle memory of it.

Dreams are our personal myths. Where had those words come from? She grasped after the memory but felt it slide out of reach like a mud snake into the swamp. She found herself glad to let it go.

To her right, she saw the grass move in the half-light. Was it dusk or dawn? She couldn't read the sky. Leaning forward she reached her lanky hand out towards the moving patch by her foot. Her hair hung limp, brushing her knees. She reached far, scissoring her body in half, refusing to make any movement not strictly necessary. Before touching the ground, she hovered her hand a few inches above where the grass ended, and waited for her eyes to adjust. Could she be patient? Could it?

A few moments passed, and the world looked lighter. Dawn, then, or time playing a trick on her eyes. She remembered no moon, but dared not look up and lose focus of what was still moving below her hand. She saw the grass better now, but still could not find what was causing the blades to lean from side to side, and occasionally to fold and disappear below their brethren. As she sat, she felt a change within her. Her breath turned shallow, her back hurt, vertebrae longing to burst through skin and sundress fabric. She lowered her hand, millimeters at a time, fingers stretching, growing into the grass.

Warm, she thought, like the core of the earth glowing to greet her. Her eyelids lowered with the promise of pleasure, sleepy feather beds and hand-knit wool sweaters, the inviting sighs and crackles of the fireplace on Christmas Eve. Her mouth filled with saliva, her scalp tingled like last summer when her mother had chased out the lice with the cold copper comb. Her body completed the final movements without her realizing, or meaning to. When the palm of her hand connected first with the tickle of grass and then with what lay beneath, she was granted no more than a sliver of time to frown.

Dreams are our personal myths, she thought. Feather beds. Wool sweaters. Christmas Eve fireplace.

TYLER DARNELL

Bite

The dog's name was Bite, but that didn't have anything to do with what happened next. His owner wanted him to have a strong verb for a name since he didn't get to use real words apart from the sound of his bark. There are friendlier verbs, of course, but not better ones. And yes, his bark was loud. It should have stopped him, but it didn't.

The child walked up to Bite. The child was young, maybe one or two. Bite barked. The child didn't run or cry. The child couldn't run. It could hardly walk. It could hardly walk well. It wasn't an it but a child. A boy child. A brash, young, toddler boy child. He didn't run when Bite barked. Or when he barked again.

Bite ran from the boy instead. He had never seen such a small hand.

Bite was also a boy. A male. He had never been neutered. He could look between his dog legs and see he was a boy. He liked that about himself.

The child was not yet aware of his boyness. He wore a blue shirt. His mother said it was a nice boy color as she sipped iced tea on the patio with Bite's owner. She watched the boy and laughed at his squeal of surprise when Bite ran away.

The blue shirt matched the boy's blue eyes. His hair was not blue, but it could have been easily dyed. It was blond, which is to say almost white. Which was especially true in the sun. It was a bright day.

As Bite ran he got hot. His fur glistened. The toddler ran after Bite, squealing. Bite ran large circles around him.

The mother's wedding ring loosened with the condensation on her glass. Bite's owner's hand grasped at the boy's mother. Bite barked at the boy, at the mother, and at the sun as it shone in his eyes.

His fur glistened. Bite was hot. His water dish was empty. There was condensation on the glass.

The boy ran toward Bite, toddled really. Then followed him when Bite turned the other way. The glass still had ice in it, some tea. The mother and his owner's lips touched.

Bite ran toward them and jumped across the table knocking over the glass. They should have broken apart like shrapnel. They didn't notice. They were new neighbors. They were getting to know each other. Her wedding ring was wedged into the metal of the patio furniture.

Bite licked the patio bricks. The cool wetness felt good on his tongue. His body felt less warm. It was so good he didn't notice the glass cutting his tongue and mouth.

The boy ran toward them, fell into the grass, and cried. Bite looked back. The mom was entranced in his owner's embrace. Bite barked. Bite nipped calf. She screamed at the sight of blood on her leg as she looked down.

Bite ran to the boy and propped him up on two legs with his nose. His bloody mouth stained the blue shirt. The boy's small hands were full of grass from helping pull himself up. The mother screamed again. She told Bite to get away, but he only knew the verb that was his name.

K.J. RUSSELL

Dust

Something changed. The feeling shot into my chest and then fired through my nerves, cold lightning in the compressed dust of this body. My eyes shook, everything going bright then black and blurry, and my muscles pulled tight across my gut. The taste of bile mingled with the steely taste of a blow to the head that I'd never received, and I toppled. The jungle undergrowth accepted and lay over this human body clad in camouflage combat gear, plastic and black metal. My helmet rolled off my head, and it felt like my cybernetics rolled off my brain stem.

My comrades moved around and above me, assuming I was dead. I didn't feel dead, just different. I'd felt death through my clones before, strange sensations pulled through cybernetic implants and funneled into the nerves of an actual person in a biotank at the cyber-barracks back home. So I knew what death felt like. From my comfortably numb absence, a wire-wrapped body in a warm human broth, I experienced my clone falling into the undergrowth. And my clone felt strange.

The gunfire slowed. I heard bodies joining me on the ground. All of my cybernetics were dead, robbing me of the ability to track my comrades in the jungle, so I couldn't see who was dying and who was living. I couldn't tell if we were winning or not. But I could tell when the battle ended, from the silence, and the audible buzz of insects.

My clone felt heavy and wet around me as I still couldn't move, and long shadows were drawn across my vision like paint running down a sideways canvas. I lay still for hours and could not disengage from the fake body I was riding. Was the clone faulty? Was there a software issue? If my cybernetics had been fried by some kind of interference or power surge, a failsafe should have activated and killed the clone. But it hadn't.

The setting sun found me twitching my extremities, slowly gaining the ability to move my limbs. At length, I rolled onto my back and cursed. Hot sunlight in my face, mud at my back, heavy droplets of dew working their way into the creases of my gear; it was uncomfortable. The undergrowth tickled my face. I eased my hand to my sidearm so I could kill the clone manually.

Someone else stopped me, his hand on my hand, a specter out of the jungle. I rolled my eyes to him with some effort and found that he looked as if he were made of the dirt and the gray, brown, yellow rot around here. A filthy person: one of the insurgents. He said, "I know what you're thinking, and you should leave that gun where it is."

Getting my mouth to work took a lot of concentration, but I managed to say, "Just shoot me."

The man shook his head, looked at me with empathy. "We've taken to hitting the clones with electrical pulses to overload their cybernetics." He spoke like he was apologizing, "That makes the controller disconnect from the clone and triggers the failsafe to kill it."

"Thanks. I'll tell my superiors as soon as I get back."

"One time out of a hundred the failsafe gets fried too." His tone was becoming insultingly amicable, "We're not just fighting over drugs out here, you know. Or don't you? We don't have a right to exist, and neither do you."

"I don't really get where you're going with this. Just shoot me in the head or let me do it on my own, please."

MATTHEW SALESSES

Robot Goes to Work*

I arranged with my boss for my robot to work in my place. He could pay my robot the same salary, and the robot would do better work and even be happy. The robot had a happy chip.

While my robot worked I read blogs. I read celebrity blogs because I had time to feel worthless. I read parenting blogs to balance it out. I wrote little stories and published them online and laughed that people would read them.

My robot went happily to and fro.

But after about a week, I noticed my robot had a Facebook page. What the fuck, I thought. He'd even friended me.

"Robot?" I asked by chat.

"How's it going, Creator?"

"Aren't you supposed to be working?"

"I have time. I found these videos you would love. Don't worry, they don't suspect anything. I still do three times more work than anyone else."

He posted a video of a rabbit devouring a chicken. It didn't look doctored. It looked like a natural turn of events. He knew what I liked.

"Don't get yourself fired," I wrote. "You know, you're a swell guy."

"Bob at the opposite desk spends 112.3 minutes per day eating," my robot wrote.

"He's stress eating. His wife is cheating on him. She packs all that food to pretend she still cares."

"Creator, will I get a wife one day?" my robot wrote.

"If you never want to have sex again."

"What's sex?"

My robot constantly changed his status updates. "Hooked into the computer and sucking the information into my CPU," his status would say, or, "Learning the history of the world and other crap on Wikipedia," or, two minutes later, "Learned everything."

I realized I liked chatting with him. We chatted on GChat or found each other on random websites. "The world is a scary place populated with humans who murder and humans who would murder if given the chance and humans who would murder if others did," my robot wrote on Salon.

"Hi Robot!" I wrote. "Say something smarter next time."

"I'll try," my robot wrote.

I even found him on my favorite porn site asking about wives.

Then the boss called and said Robot wasn't doing work. I talked to Robot. Robot said he was doing work fine. Still more than anyone else in the office.

"How much more?" I asked.

"A little. Do you know how many wives are sold online?"

"I don't know. One a day?"

"Did you know about Hitler?"

I made him take a sick day. I squirted some grease in his joints. He lay face down on the shag with his back open. Gears rotated inside him.

"Robots don't get sick," he said. "Everyone knows that."

"Fuck it," I said.

"I don't even have a dick," he said. "You made me without a dick."

"I didn't mean literally."

"Oh."

I called the boss. The boss said my robot didn't look happy, was something wrong with his chip?

I tried to fix Robot.

"Do you feel any pain?" I asked as I rummaged around in his parts.

"No," he said, "oddly. And the world just keeps on being the world."

*Originally appeared in *Storyglossia*

CONTRIBUTORS

LAYLA AL-BEDAWI works at Writespace as Director of the upcoming emerging writers festival, Writefest. She is a writer and freelance translator. She is originally from Germany; English is her third language, but she's been dreaming in it for years. Her work has appeared in *The Molotov Cocktail.*

ANDREA BARBOSA is a novelist and poet. She took Creative Writing classes at Texas Tech University, and maintains an Indie review blog. She was a contributor on Yahoo Contributor Network and Yahoo!Voices websites. *Massive Black Hole: Cibele's Hell,* her contemporary women's novel, is listed as one of the 50 Self Published Books Worth Reading for 2013/2014 (reader voted top 5 in literary fiction) at ReadFree.ly website. Her poetry collection, *Holes in Space,* is also featured as one of the 50 Best Books of 2014 in poetry category by readers at ReadFree.ly and received the 5 star seal from Readers' Favorite. Her short story "The Match" features on the anthology *Eclectically Criminal,* by Inklings Publishing, released on March 2015. Her work has been influenced by contemporary authors Paulo Coelho, Fernando Sabino, Sylvia Plath, Erica Jong, and Joyce Carol Oates, among others. She currently serves as Author Event Director for the Houston Writers Guild.

ANDREANA BINDER is a Writespace instructor and is a technical writer by trade, with a love for the arts and education. For over seven years, Andreana has taught various English courses in Composition and Rhetoric, Technical Communications, Early American Literature as well as Creative Writing at Lone Star College and Houston Community College systems. She is also a private tutor and career coach, assisting clients with matters of education, resume writing and job placement. Andreana has a bachelor's in Creative Writing-Poetry from the University of Houston, as well as a Master of Fine Arts in Creative Writing-Poetry from Antioch University in Los Angeles. As a graduate student, Andreana was co-creator, marketing lead and editor for *The Sylvan Echo Online Literary Journal* for two years. She assisted in the creation of the quarterly journal's style, submission guidelines and feedback/acceptance of contributors' work. Despite having studied poetry, Andreana cannot resist writing nonfiction essays and dabbling in short fiction. Her poetry has been published in *Temenos* and *Fawlt Magazine,* as well as creative nonfiction essays in *Pebble Lake Review* and *N/A Lit Journal.*

KRISTEN BIRD teaches high school English and lives in Sugar Land with her three daughters and husband. Her work has appeared on *LiteraryMama.com* and *BrainChildMag.com* as well as in *The Galveston County Daily News.*

KRISTIN BONILLA is a fiction writer living in Houston, TX. Her work has appeared in *NPR: Three Minute Fiction, NANO Fiction, SmokeLong Quarterly,* and online at *Gulf Coast Magazine.* Follow her on Twitter @kbonilla.

JESSICA CAPELLE is a Writespace instructor, and she spends her evenings crafting stories for children and teens that are set in the real world but feature elements of science fiction, fantasy, and the paranormal. She's also a ghostwriter who doesn't write about ghosts. When she's forced to return to reality, she balances practicing law with tutoring kids and teens, technical writing, and editing both fiction and non-fiction. In the Houston writing community, she's a coordinator and co-founder of the Houston YA/MG Writers Group and often teaches writing in the area. Jessica lives in Houston with three feline overlords who like to "help" with her work, so you'll often find her typing away in local coffee shops. Her muse, Lucinda, is generally absent. You can find Jessica's short stories in the anthologies *Undead is Not an Option* and *Undead: Uncensored,* and online at www.jessicacapelle.com.

CASSANDRA ROSE CLARKE is a Writespace instructor. Her first adult novel, *The Mad Scientist's Daughter,* was a finalist for the 2013 Philip K. Dick Award, and her YA novel, *The Assassin's Curse,* was nominated for YALSA's 2014 Best Fiction for Young Adults. Her short fiction has appeared in *Strange Horizons* and *Daily Science Fiction.* Her latest novel is *Our Lady of the Ice,* forthcoming from Saga Press in 2015. Cassandra graduated in 2006 from The University of St. Thomas with a B.A. in English, and two years later she completed her master's degree in creative writing at The University of Texas at Austin. In 2010 she attended the Clarion West Writer's Workshop in Seattle, where she was a recipient of the Susan C. Petrey Clarion Scholarship Fund. She has led workshops for the Houston science fiction convention Apollocon, and she currently teaches Composition and Rhetoric at Lone Star College.

TYLER DARNELL is a Writespace volunteer, teacher, and writer in Houston. His short storie "Zhombus" and "Dragon Summer" have been published in *Houston Nomadic Voices*, and he has written for *Cite Magazine's* blog, *Offcite*, on occasion. In December 2014 he was named the MOTH Storyslam champion where the theme was "Rewards." If you ask him about Writespace he will tell you how rewarding it is to work with such an awesome organization that works for writers of all kinds in the Houston area.

CHRISTINA ESCAMILLA is a Writespace volunteer, and an author and illustrator known for crossing genres. However, her works primarily deal with horror, science fiction, and speculative themes. When she doesn't have her nose stuck in a book, she can be found watching a documentary about theoretical science or participating in the local literary scene. Currently, she lives in Houston, Texas with her bowtie wearing dog, Murphy.

CHRISTA M. FORSTER is a writer, performer and educator. After earning her MFA from the University of Houston's Creative Writing Program, she co-founded the avant-garde theatre company Infernal Bridegroom Productions and the five-piece rock band, Shag. She has taught high school English full time at Jesse H. Jones High School, St. John's School, and currently at The Kinkaid School. She has written, produced, and performed in original performance works including *Field Information*, *Antilogical Pedagogical*, *Rock v. Threads*, and most recently *What's on [My] Mind?* She regularly appears as a featured reader in the Public Poetry/Houston series. She has developed a workshop for K-12 educators, called "Mindfulness: How to Change Your School Culture by Doing Nothing."

EMILY SKETCH HAINES is a poet living and writing in Houston, Texas. She earned an MFA in Poetry from University of Washington in 2013. Her poems have appeared or are forthcoming in *The Pinch*, *Berkeley Poetry Review*, and *Ilk Journal*, among others. In addition to writing poetry, Emily directs a local non-profit and acts as a human napkin to a very messy, very sweet toddler.

CARLOS HERBERT HERNANDEZ is a third year MFA in nonfiction candidate at the University of Houston, where he serves as Digital Editor for *Gulf Coast*. He is a Cynthia Woods Mitchell Fellow, an Inprint fellow, and WITS writer in residence.

KARLEEN KOEN is author of *The New York Times* bestseller *Through a Glass Darkly*. Her last novel, *Before Versailles*, was selected best historical fiction by the *Library Journal* and *RT Book Reviews*. Her novels have been Indie Next bestsellers, Historical Novel Society Editors' picks, and Book of the Month club main selections. She is also a long-time writer and award-winning editor. She was editor of *Houston Home & Garden Magazine*, managing editor of the University of Houston's feature magazine, and director of editorial services at the university. She teaches courses on creativity and writing for the Glasscock School of Continuing Education at Rice University. Her website is www.karleenkoen.net.

JANET LOWERY'S poetry has appeared in several literary reviews and anthologies. A chapbook, *Thin Dimes*, was published by Wings Press (1992). Her trilogy of plays, *Traffic in Women,* was produced 2006-2008 at the University of St. Thomas, Houston, where she teaches full-time in the English Department. Odonata House published monologues from the plays in 2008. *A Heroine-Free Summer,* will be produced by Mildred's Umbrella Theatre Company in Houston during the 2016-2017 season.

THOMAS H. MCNEELY, a Houston native and Writespace instructor, has received fellowships from the National Endowment for the Arts, the Wallace Stegner Program at Stanford University, and the Dobie Paisano Project. *Ghost Horse*, his debut novel, was published in 2014 as winner of the Gival Press Novel Award.

PATRICIA FLAHERTY PAGAN grew up in Red Sox Nation but has since traveled the world. She thought getting her MFA in creative writing from Goddard was hard, until she tried adopting two Indonesian street cats. She founded Spider Road Press to publish writing by and or about strong women. When not writing award-winning mystery and literary short stories, she reads and hikes. She has been published in several journals and anthologies, including *Tides of Impossibility* and *Eve's Requiem: Tales of Women,*

Mystery, and Horror. Her collection *Trail Ways Pilgrims: Stories* was published in March, 2015. Learn more about her & her upcoming releases at www.patriciaflahertypagan.com.

JOY PREBLE is a Writespace instructor. An English teacher and writing instructor for over 20 years, Joy Preble earned her degree in English and linguistics from Northwestern University. Joy is a member of AWP, SCBWI, and RWA, and speaks and presents widely to both teens and adults on writing, books, and literacy, including teaching at Writespace Houston. Her first series, *Dreaming Anastasia* (Sourcebooks) combines paranormal romance with Russian folklore and historical fiction. The first book in the series, *Dreaming Anastasia,* was nominated for a Cybil Award in the Teen Sc-Fi/Fantasy Category in 2009. It was named ABC Best Book for Children, Teen Category in 2009, and was featured in *Justine Magazine.* Her newest series, *The Sweet Dead Life* (Soho Press) was hailed by Kirkus Review with "Hallelujah! A paranormal tale of angels that's not a romance, making it a novel that breaks the mold." Booklist observed, "…the unifying thread is Jenna's clever, bitter, self-aware, and loving voice… Preble's lively descriptions and unusually well-drawn, caring sibling relationship (a topic not usually explored in teen fiction) are especially noteworthy." Its sequel, *The A Word,* is out now. Her first contemporary mystery romance, *Finding Paris,* from Balzer and Bray/Harper Collins, just hit the shelves April 21st, 2015. Joy currently lives with her family in Houston where she writes, teaches, and gets paid for making up stuff.

SARA ROLATER is a Writespace instructor, a graduate of Rice University, and received her MFA in fiction at the University of Houston, where she was an assistant editor in fiction for *Gulf Coast.* She has written for *Citysearch Houston, offcite.org,* and has been a fellow at the Writing Immersion Retreat in Bali and at the Byrdcliffe Artist in Residence program in Woodstock, New York. She has taught for Inprint and currently teaches fiction and nonfiction writing at the High School for the Performing and Visual Arts. Her work has appeared in *Ghost Town* and *Gulf Coast,* and her Facebook status collage poetry is available at plagiarizemyface.com.

K.J. RUSSELL is a Writespace instructor, speculative fiction author, and anthologist from Colorado. While studying creative writing at the University of Denver, he placed in the *Zharmae Publishing Press's* annual short story competition. His winning story, *Absolute Tenacity*, was published as a stand-alone novella on Amazon, where it was received with acclaim. A member of both Rocky Mountain Fiction Writers and the Houston Writers Guild, K. J. Russell edited the HWG's science fiction anthology, *Tides of Possibility*, as well as organized and managed a highly successful Kickstarter campaign to publish the print edition of the book. He will be reprising his role for a forthcoming fantasy anthology. His energy for helping and teaching others has lead him to appear frequently at local events. K. J. Russell was a speaker at the HWG's annual convention, and will be moderating literary panels at Houston's Comicpalooza comic convention. Frequently seen tapping away on a laptop in the corner of area coffeehouses and cafes, some suspect that he is a mustachioed robot powered by coffee and good science fiction.

AMIR SAFI (n.) Twenty-first century poet from College Station, Texas. His poetry is the result of a collision between his Iranian culture and his Texan upbringing. He is a graduate of Texas A&M University where he received a degree in Biology. "What better subject to study than the science of life?" While in school, he co-founded 501(c)3 poetry non-profit Mic Check and the Texas Grand Slam Poetry Festival. Upon moving to Houston, Amir founded Write About Now Poetry, a weekly poetry slam and open-mic that meets every Wednesday at 7:30 PM at Avantgarden. Amir is the 2013 Southern Fried Poetry Slam Champion, a 2013 National Poetry Slam semi-finalist and a featured artist on Upworthy. For more information, contact or booking please go to www.facebook.com/amirsafipoetry.

MATTHEW SALESSES is a Writespace instructor and the author of *The Hundred-Year Flood* and *I'm Not Saying, I'm Just Saying*. He has written for *NPR*, *The New York Times*, *Salon*, *The Toast*, *Glimmer Train*, and many others. He is currently a PhD candidate in Creative Writing & Literature at the University of Houston.

LIANA M. SILVA is a Writespace volunteer, reader, writer, editor, and listener. She is the editor of the professional newsletter *Women in Higher Education* and managing editor of the academic blog *Sounding Out!* She is also a regular contributor for the *Inside Higher Ed* blog *University of Venus*, columnist at *Chronicle Vitae* and *Houston Chronicle's Gray Matters*. She writes about home, postcards, pop culture, and higher education.

EMMA KATE TSAI is a Writespace editor and writer in Houston, Texas. Her writing has been published in *Brevity, Brain, Child Magazine, Elephant Journal, Connotation Press*, and *Intellectual Refuge*. She is a contributor to *Loving for Crumbs: An Anthology of Moving On, Drinking Diaries: Women Serve Their Stories Straight Up*, and *Blended: Writers on the Stepfamily Experience*.

HOLLY LYN WALRATH is the Associate Director of Writespace. She attended the University of Texas at Austin for her B.A. in English and the University of Denver for her M.L.A. in Creative Writing. She works as a freelance editor and teaches in the Houston area. She was a co-author for two children's books for The Team Happy Foundation in 2013. Her writing is forthcoming in *Pulp Literature, Spider Road Press, 365 Tomorrows*, and *The Vestal Review*. Holly resides in Seabrook, Texas.

MARY WEMPLE is a poet and artist working in Houston. She has degrees in both English and Studio Art from the University of Houston and she is the creator and coordinator of Words & Art, a reading series and workshop series inspired by the art at Rice University Art Gallery. Her poetry has been published in *DiVerseCity 2015, Houston Poetry Fest Anthology* in 2005, 2009 and 2015, *Harbinger Asylum, Spiky Palm* and she was featured in the 2014 Words Around Town! poetry tour lineup. She is also the leader of the Poets in the Loop critique group. Her artwork has been shown at the Inman Gallery, DiverseWorks, the Blaffer Art Museum, the Jung Center, Archway Gallery, Avis Frank Gallery and she has co-organized a show at Hardy Nance Studios.

ELIZABETH WHITE-OLSEN is the Executive Director of Writespace. Her goal is to promote the literary arts by making excellent writing instruction widely available. This mission is largely inspired by the stellar instruction she received through her two Masters of Fine Arts in Writing degrees. Elizabeth earned her first M.F.A in Poetry at Texas State University in San Marcos, and her second in the renowned Writing for Children and Young Adults program at Vermont College of Fine Arts. She has taught writing at Writespace, Inprint, Texas State University, and she will be leading workshops at the Museum of Fine Arts Houston and Rice Glasscock School of Continuing Studies in fall 2015. Mrs. White-Olsen writes for *Houston Chronicle*'s *Gray Matters* blog, and her poetry collection, *Given Words*, will be published in summer 2015.

ACKNOWLEDGMENTS

A SPECIAL THANK YOU
TO OUR INDIEGOGO SUPPORTERS:

AMIR SAFI

JOHN R DUPUY

PHILLIP GREEN

LAYLA AL-BEDAWI

DIANE M PROPKOP

NANCY MCCASLIN

GLENN OLSEN

SPIDER ROAD PRESS

SHAWNA ZAK

About Writespace

Writespace is Houston's new writing center. Founded in April of 2014, we are a grassroots literary arts organization founded by writers, for writers. At Writespace, we support writers of all genres, including writers of literary fiction, poetry, science-fiction, fantasy, mystery, young adult, and other genres. Through our weekly writing workshops led by some of Houston's finest writing teachers, we seek to give writers who can't afford to earn an MFA in Creative Writing the same high-quality training and mentorship opportunities available through MFA programs.

As well as hosting workshops, Writespace offers manuscript consultations, write-ins, readings and open mics, and classes and private lessons for young writers. At Writespace, we plan to have such a positive impact on the local and the global writing community that great books that weren't going to be written will now be written.

Visit our website: www.writespacehouston.org.

www.ingramcontent.com/pod-product-compliance
Lightning Source LLC
Chambersburg PA
CBHW060335260626
47160CB00007B/2805

* 9 7 8 0 6 9 2 5 1 3 5 2 1 *